THE ...
D...

GRAHAM COX

PERNICE
PRESS

First published in the UK in 2014 by Pernice Press

British Library Cataloguing in Publication data

A catalogue record for this book is available from the British Library

ISBN 978 0 9926275 1 5

Book design by Matt Swann Creative Ltd
21stBookDesign.blogspot.com

Printed and bound in Great Britain by
CPI Antony Rowe, Chippenham, Wiltshire

PERNICE PRESS
27 Cambrian Road
Richmond, Surrey TW10 6JQ, United Kingdom
www.pernicepress.com

Contents

INTRODUCTION:
IN PRAISE OF SMALL THINGS

T HAT 'THE BEST THINGS come in small packages' is something I have always believed. Amongst the many, many thousands of pages written about the education of gundogs just 25, for me, stand out as very special. Together they make up Vincent Routledge's 'Little Red Book', *The Ideal Retriever and How to Handle Him*, first published in 1929.

In it Routledge, who assumes that someone else will be doing the training, sets out in words which are as succinct as they are clear the priorities which should guide the training process and the handling of a dog that has been appropriately educated.

The ideal retriever, he says, "must have a really highly developed sense of smell to enable him to gallop on the line of a runner when scent is good, and to hunt it out inch by inch when scent is almost non-existent … He must have determination and perseverance to enable him to find game in spite of every difficulty; to face cover and water no matter how thick or cold; he must never give up hope, but keep trying until called in … He must be a good marker, go quickly to the 'fall' … before attempting to hunt further afield. His mouth should be of velvet, incapable of mouthing a bird when retrieving to hand, and last, but not least, he must have brains, without which he is never likely to be first class."

Those words could be equally well applied to any breed of gundog, and field sportsmen and women who have any awareness of the ethical implications of their activities should aspire to being accompanied by such a dog. Of course, anything approximating Routledge's 'ideal' would be a fine thing, and the belief that underpins this little book is that such an admirable aspiration is attainable by anyone prepared to give it their best shot. It sets out to show what Routledge delegated to others, namely the craft skills you will need to acquire if you are to nurture the qualities that he so clearly describes.

Just one year before Routledge published his lucid essay the novelist Virginia Woolf published her plea that women's creative abilities might take wing in *A Room of One's Own*. Reflecting on her task in her opening chapter she acknowledged 'one fatal drawback' in her project. "I should never", she wrote, "be able to fulfil what is, I understand, the first duty of a lecturer — to hand you after an hour's discourse a nugget of pure truth to wrap up between the pages of your notebooks and keep on the mantelpiece for ever."

Well, after a lifetime in Higher Education, it is an ambition I still take seriously. This little book is conceived as a workbook: one to be returned to again and again during the education process. Its brevity is testament to the fact that it focuses on priorities and, more than that, it unashamedly sets out to offer a good many 'nuggets of pure truth' to act as beacons, lode stars, signposts even, as we navigate the journey which the education of any gundog is sure to entail.

Considerable strides have been made in the training of dogs, and the days when people routinely spoke and wrote of 'breaking' dogs to the gun are thankfully well behind us. And yet we cannot afford to be complacent because the misconceived impulse to seek a 'technical fix' for the challenges inevitably encountered is ever present.

This book seeks to draw on the insights and craft skills which could be presumed in the 'world we have lost' whilst combining them with the best informed contemporary thoughts about gundog training. My fondest hope, though, is that its pages will encourage you to think and reflect on the process and, perhaps even, find your own way. That's certainly a realistic ambition: but only you can make it a reality.

SECTION I

WHAT YOU NEED

There is much you should consider before acquiring a dog and training it for the shooting field. Ethical imperatives demand that we shoot over competent dogs and nothing matters more than having a clear sense of what that means. So, get a feel for the overall shape of the education process and what can be achieved. Core principles really matter, as does your mindset. Be ready always to blame yourself for setbacks and be prepared to go backwards to go forwards.

The nature of that education process will, of course, be much affected by what you are working with. For, whatever your favoured breed, strong evidence of working ability in your dog's parentage will enhance the potential for success. And such success is a realistic aspiration. Indeed, 'if you don't accept second best you'll get the best'. But first you have to know what the best looks like.

A TRAINING PHILOSOPHY

A KEY REASON WHY, for all its brevity, Vincent Routledge's book is so valuable is that it presents us with an utterly clear sense of what a finished dog should look like. Nothing is more important, when setting out to train a gundog, than an uncluttered appreciation of the likely nature of the process and the hoped for outcome.

So often we find ourselves having to go back to go forward in order to embed more thoroughly an aspect of the process which has proved to be insufficiently understood. At such times having a good sense of overall direction is vital. Producing an agreeable shooting companion requires, of course, that we add application to that understanding of the overall process. Doing that is well within the compass of anyone with sufficient commitment. We want our dog to be steady, a precondition for its being able to work in a controlled manner. But above all we want it to be an effective hunter so that it is capable of finding game and recovering it after it has been shot.

The overriding imperative is the ethical one of being capable of retrieving wounded game as expeditiously as possible and a dog able to do that effectively will be an asset on any shoot. Indeed, there is no more satisfying sequence than proving to be the equal of a really sporting bird and having a dog which can bring it stylishly to hand with a minimum of fuss.

Anything can be done well or less well, and that's why that word 'stylishly' is so important. Work which is more than merely functionally effective lifts the spirits: and that is something that sportsmen have always keenly appreciated. One of the most celebrated, Colonel Thornton, for instance, wrote in his *Sporting Tour Through The Northern Parts of England and Great Part of the Highlands of Scotland* published in 1804: "I conceive that the great pleasure and elegance of shooting depends on the good order in which the dogs are kept." Although Thornton was writing about walking up grouse over pointers his observation is as relevant to the circumstances of game shooting now as it was two centuries and more ago. 'Pleasure and elegance' are certainly worth striving for: not least because they can raise sport from the mundane to the life-enhancing.

The first concern of any shooter or picker-up must be to get wounded game collected quickly and humanely despatched and a competent gundog is essential to that task. But the performance of that task can be so much more, and if we keep in mind the adage that 'if you don't accept second best you'll get the best', it can be. Educating a gundog is all about achieving 'good order' and that, in turn, depends on the sequence in which you do things, the degree to which you do them and the manner in which you do them. This book aims to make those essentials really clear so that you are never in any doubt about the direction you are taking. It should also be emphasised that the core principles will instil confidence: a vital precondition for success in almost any enterprise.

There is no royal road to training a gundog and I hope you will be creative in your approach to the process. If you think critically about the progress you are making in the light of the principles which this book emphasises this is likely to happen. So often that progress depends on absorbing elements of a distinctive culture rather than slavishly adhering to sets of instructions: but it has to be within the framework provided by fundamental truths which are essential to success.

In another context the nineteenth century American poet and essayist Ralph Waldo Emerson made the point brilliantly. "As to methods", he suggested, "there may be a million, and then some; but principles are few. The man who grasps principles can successfully select his own methods. The man who tries methods, ignoring principles, is sure to have trouble." Those are wise words indeed; and they apply with particular force to what must happen during the education of a gundog.

So there are good reasons why this small book repeats certain key points. They are few in number, but their constant revision is essential to success because they must always be in mind. That is why each section of the book will have an introductory summary and, at its end, a series of bullet points which warrant particular attention. I'll also be trying, whenever possible, to offer easy shorthand ways of committing key points to memory. This is intended to be a workbook which can easily be kept at hand so that it can be dipped into whenever necessary to refresh appreciation of those priorities.

More often than not books about gundog training have been written by people who have competed successfully with their dogs for people who are presumed to entertain such aspirations. This book assumes no such ambition. Its focus is not on gundog working tests or, still less, field trials. It is organised and written solely with the gun who wishes to have a competent shooting companion in mind. The hope, rather, is that its succinctness and emphasis on key principles will make it possible for the reader always to have the whole wood in view and never find themselves befuddled by a thicket of trees.

Someone once characterised the training process in terms of a simple equation, suggesting that it was Education + Application − Confusion. That last element, confusion, is to be avoided at all costs. There is no better precept than the one which encourages you to 'always blame yourself'. The first impulse, when a dog is struggling, should be to ask what it is that it doesn't understand adequately. That is why making progress, and going forward, so often involves going back to make sure that some earlier lesson has been thoroughly understood. The greatest asset of British gundogs is their responsiveness and general biddability. Generally they are not, in fact, looking to be recalcitrant so if confusion is evident steps have to be taken to resolve it. Some inadequacy in the education process has been highlighted and it must be rectified.

Adopt that mindset and you will have every chance of succeeding. How you think about the adventure that you have embarked on with your pup, of whatever breed, will have a huge bearing on your enjoyment of the process. If you approach the educative process with clarity and in a nurturing way there is every chance that your dog will respond in like manner and, so long as you work at it, you will become a cooperative and mutually supportive team. It is the aim of this book to make that outcome much more, rather than less, likely.

Choosing a Shooting Companion

As long ago as 1891, when driven shooting was in its infancy, F R Bevan in the 4th Edition of his *Observations on Breaking Retrievers* wrote: "I have constantly remarked that men who shoot without dogs tire of sport early in life, whilst all who are fond of animals and of training them retain a long lasting pleasure in it." He had a point. More than that, though, ethical considerations — always a priority — are now more pressing than ever. The recovery of wounded game is the first obligation of any sportsman and a trained gundog is essential to that task.

So, there are good reasons why the impulse to get a dog and train it yourself is a strong one. But giving substance to that worthy ambition should prompt a host of questions: most importantly, which breed? Answering that question involves thinking carefully about the sort of shooting that you principally do. After all, the breeds best suited to lone rough shooting forays may not be ideally suited as peg dogs on a heavy driven day. That isn't an absolute matter, though, and liking for a breed — the desire to own and work one — is a really important consideration because you are far more likely to establish a good working relationship with a dog that you feel a natural affinity towards. The absolute last thing to suppose, however, is that merely by acquiring a particular breed of dog your problems are solved. It's what you do with them that really matters.

There are no fewer than 36 gundog breeds, divided principally into four groups: retrievers, spaniels, pointers and setters and dogs which hunt, point and retrieve (HPRs). The numbers of dogs in the various breeds vary very widely. So, for instance, you may yearn to own and work a Field Spaniel. But, in 2012, just 47 were registered whereas the corresponding figure for by far the most numerous of the gundog breeds, the Labarador Retriever, was 36,487. Of the spaniels cockers are by far the most numerous with 23,306 registrations as against 12,792 springers. In retrievers, meanwhile — and to put that towering labrador total in perspective — there were 7,085 goldens and 1,184 flatcoats. In HPRs, where German Shorthaired Pointers and Hungarian Vizslas dominate, their numbers were 1,225 and 1,607 respectively.

These totals, of course, are just that. They include dogs bred purely with showing in mind, whereas you will want to want to acquire a pup whose ancestors have consistently shown an ability to work and the figures do effectively indicate how easy or not it might be to do that. That matters because with breeding we are in the realm of probabilities and you will want to maximise the chance that the dog you acquire will exhibit certain key traits which add up to trainability.

Everything depends on what you do with the dog, but your own efforts will have a huge impact on its biddability and responsiveness; and nothing matters more, because that will to please makes the education process so much more enjoyable for you and your dog. And, as we've seen time and again, dogs can be trained to do almost anything. So, although spaniels are most at home hunting and flushing they can make effective peg dogs; and whilst labradors are best suited to sitting at a drive they can, just as effectively, hunt up a hedgerow. The moral is clear. In choosing a shooting companion, follow your inclination and make it work.

Working Breeding Matters

WHATEVER SHOOTING YOU'RE LUCKY enough to do one thing's for sure: having a well-trained and responsive gundog with you will enormously enhance the experience as well as increasing the chances of recovering wounded game; and there's nothing more important than that.

Those two words, well-trained and responsive, are crucial though. Because an untrained dog on a shooting day is not just irritating, it's worse than useless. Training is an ongoing thing, so even if you entrust some of it to a professional, it's mostly going to be down to you. The same goes for responsiveness, though here it matters more than somewhat just what you start out with. If there is one quality which working bred British gundogs have it is biddability: the potential to become companionable gamefinders.

Again, potential is the operative word. Working breeding is how you get it: whether or not it's realised is another matter. But let's begin at the beginning. If you are going to get a dog, what considerations should be uppermost? The breed you choose should be determined principally by your preference and the sort of shooting that you do, though that's less important because dogs can be trained to do almost anything. An English Springer Spaniel may not be cut out to be a peg dog, but many are and what matters most is that you get on with your dog, enjoy being with it and feel positively about its capabilities. Enthusiasm counts for a lot: for both of you, so lukewarm relationships are best avoided.

If most of your shooting is driven it would make sense to have a preference for a Labrador or Golden Retriever. And then you'll need to look carefully at whatever preconceptions you may have: because, as with most things, mythologies abound. And invariably they fall into the 'snare and delusion' category. Shooting men have long been inclined to disparage dogs that are 'on the whistle' until, that is, something needs doing which only dogs under such control can accomplish. Then the flip flop switches to fulsome praise mode. Neither is appropriate.

The fact is that work at field trials, for that is what is being scoffed at, is in H W Carlton's immortal words written almost a century ago, "only work in the field brought to a state more nearly bordering on perfection." But what of the canard that trial dogs are too hot? Well, certainly if you start with a line-bred working Labrador you may, as it were, be driving an Aston Martin rather than a reconditioned Morris Minor. But it is up to you to be equal to the challenges and the possibilities that presents. It is surely more admirable to resolve to acquire the necessary training skills and competences rather than accept second best and fondly suppose that, because it isn't supercharged, your shooting companion can be left to train itself on the job. That really is the greatest delusion of all.

More than one great gundog name of the past — John Kent, Joe Greatorex and Keith Erlandson come to mind — can lay claim to the perceptive observation that "the bane of the gundog world is poor well-bred bitches mated to good or fashionable sires". The ease of communication these days has only accentuated that tendency, and anyone who has been shooting for longer than five minutes will have seen plenty of dogs that tick those boxes. So, what does a well-bred gundog look like? I'm not talking appearance: rather, what the dog looks like on paper; what its lineage tells you about its potential, its likely capabilities.

Breeding matters. The competence of trainers and handlers is vital, but breeding is the bedrock. It's all about probabilities, of course, and chance can never be eliminated. There are time-honoured rules of thumb, certainly, but successful breeding demands more than their routine application. The exercise of flair and imagination is a necessity and the gift of a 'feel' for the way that bloodlines might or might not 'nick' is not given to everyone. The principle which lies behind line breeding is often characterised as 'breed the best to the best and hope for the best'. But hope is the key word, and its beguiling simplicity conceals the judgement needed to achieve the best consistently.

Gary Johnson and Dr Isabelle Kraft published their third volume of Labrador Champions in 2010, covering the period 1999–2009, and the details of the 190 Field Trial Champions — 108 black dogs, 47 black bitches, 20 yellow dogs and 15 yellow bitches — speak with a clear message at a time when breeding practices are so often subjected to ill-informed criticism. This invaluable work of reference is effectively a hymn to line-breeding, as Joy Venturi-Rose's essay on the development and history of the last decade's FTChs makes clear.

In these days of motorway travel prominent sires have every chance to consolidate their influence. None has been more significant than David Garbutt's 1991 Retriever Champion FTCh Pocklea Remus. Between 1993 and 2005 dogs sired by him qualified for the Retriever Championship 54 times, a figure almost double that achieved by the next most significant Championship sire, FTCh Greenwood Timothy of Holdgate.

Remus, whelped in 1986, was out of Drakeshead Gypsy who David Garbutt had handled into third place in the 1984 Championship at Stratfield Saye, and by FTCh Haretor Mark of Drakeshead. Both carried lines, on both their sires' and dams' sides, to FTCh Swinbrook Tan; himself sire of 15 FTChs and two Championship winners. The influence of Mark and his son Remus is exceptional, but as Joy shows FTCh Aughacasla Sam of Drakeshead has, amongst others like FTChs Holdgate Willie and Tibea Tosh, been important too. This Irish import, by Ballyellery Adder and out of Irish FTCh Killerisk Hero, was the sire of Tom Smith's 2001 Retriever Champion FTCh Craighorn Bracken.

The vast majority of the FTChs in the volume have these lines in their five generation pedigree and, more often than not, show some degree of line breeding onto these three dogs. The winner of the centenary Championship in 2009, for instance, the Duchess of Devonshire's FTCh Roberto Rannaldini of Bolton Abbey, is by FTCh Pocklea Adder, a son of Remus. His grand-dam on his sire's side, meanwhile, is a daughter of Sam put to Middlegate Dash, a Mark daughter.

Bitches do not have the same opportunity to prove their worth as producers, yet their significance is, if anything, enhanced with many holding that quality comes principally through the bitch line. John and Sandra Halstead outline some breeding strategies and talk, in particular, about why they mated their foundation bitch Dipper of Drakeshead to FTCh Swinbrook Tan. She was a daughter of FTCh Sendhurst Sweep, who had won the Retriever Championship in 1965 and again in 1968, and the mating emphasised both that line and the bitch line to FTCh Ruro Snipe. This dog was campaigned by Arnold White-Robinson who won the Pointer and Setter Championship five times and the Retriever Championship twice for the Duke of Wellington. The resulting litter included five outstanding dogs, amongst them two influential sires.

The bitch line from FTCh Glenpatrick Halo, a Remus daughter, has proved very successful. Put to Steve Jolly's 1998 Retriever Champion FTCh Garendon Captain, for instance, she produced FTCh Glenpatrick Eve who has herself produced numbers of FTChs when put to FTCh Strad Benis, the 2007 Retriever Champion FTCh Willowyck Ruff and David Garbutt's FTCh Pocklea Adder.

Look where you may, excellence is never a chance matter. Periodic outcrossing can be important, of course, and Irish dogs have often proved useful in that way. Also critical to line breeding, of course, is the soundness of the stock. Health testing and certification is now more prevalent and every care should be taken in that respect. As John and Sandra Halstead make clear in a final comment, none of us knows what the future may bring: but with experience and the knowledge collected together in *Labradors 2010* we can certainly "put the odds in our favour."

That's surely the way to think about it, and the same goes if you're thinking of acquiring a new shooting companion. Take advice, take care and look for a dog with a pedigree which shows proven working quality and purpose behind the pup you are taking on.

SECTION I
SUMMARY

- YOU SHOULD, BEFORE YOU PROCEED, HAVE A CLEAR SENSE OF WHAT YOU ARE AIMING AT. SO, HAVE YOU TAKEN THE TROUBLE TO SEE SOME GOOD DOGS WORKING?

- HAVE YOU RESOLVED TO RESPOND TO SETBACKS IN THE EDUCATION PROCESS, WHICH ARE BOUND TO OCCUR, BY HONESTLY ASKING YOURSELF WHERE YOU HAVE GONE WRONG AND BEING PREPARED TO GO BACK TO GET SOMETHING RIGHT BEFORE PROCEEDING FURTHER?

- DO YOU APPRECIATE THE SIGNIFICANCE OF WORKING BREEDING FOR THE LIKELY SUCCESS OF THE JOURNEY YOU ARE ABOUT TO SET OUT ON?

Section II

How to Think About the Training Process

Nothing matters more than the general approach you adopt in seeking to educate your dog. So this section is very important. To become your dog's 'pack leader' is a worthy aim: but you need to understand what makes for effective leadership in the canine world. Domination should play no part. Keep a few time-honoured truths in mind. They will make it easier to get everything else to fall into place. Aim for a 'calm assertiveness' and never forget, whilst trying to acquire it, that trust and, above all, respect must be the absolute bedrock for your efforts. Mutual respect will be fundamental to the success of your working relationship.

So You Want to be Pack Leader?

PACK LEADER IS ONE of those graphic phrases that have become part of the mental baggage of almost everyone who sets out to train — or, as I would say, educate — a gundog. The logic of the case is familiar enough: dogs are 99.8 per cent genetically identical to grey wolves and DNA evidence suggests at least a 100,000 year relationship with humans. Dogs have an extraordinary range of special skills to interact with humans but, so the argument goes, dogs are — in a very fundamental sense — pack animals and, if we want to work effectively with them, we had better make ourselves 'pack leaders'.

The phrase comes with all kinds of cultural presumptions though, and ridding ourselves of some of the more prevalent ones may be crucial to making a good job of placing ourselves at the centre of our dog's world. Whether folk know it directly or not, a potent source of understanding about what it is to be a pack leader is likely to be Jack London's celebrated parable *The Call of the Wild*.

It centres on Buck, a previously domesticated dog, who comes to serve as a sled dog during the 19th century Klondike Gold Rush. Horrendously mistreated, he is rescued by John Thornton, who cuts him from his traces. Their bond is the closest imaginable, and when Thornton is killed by Native Americans, Buck avenges his death before returning to the woods to become the alpha wolf of the pack. Buck's physical strength is prodigious and his heart unbreakable. Indeed, so bloody are the three successive battles that enable him to establish precedence that one chapter's title, 'The Dominant Primordial Beast', is well chosen. He had learned that he must master or be mastered: while to show mercy was a weakness.

So, Buck's world is red in tooth and claw. Violence and cruelty are never far away. But, look closer and it's apparent that Buck is saved as much by his wits as by his physical prowess. Much is made of his imagination. He is quicker thinking than the others in the team and the qualities which sustain his leadership are not combative, but, rather, a matter of his excelling "in giving the law and making his mates live up to it."

That gives us a key insight into what being 'pack leader' might actually mean, and more recent research shows clearly that, even in the world of the wolf pack, effective leadership has little to do with 'biff bang pow' dominance. Although based on experience, the story of Buck is a work of fiction. In 2010, though, Shaun Ellis published *The Man Who Lives With Wolves*, recounting his attempt to connect with wolves and understand their form of life by living it himself. "Most human beings", he comments, "want to make the animals they love be more like them: I had always wanted to be more like the animals I loved." That word 'love' is not prominent in the book, though, when talking about wolves and their pack dynamics. No, the words which recur time and again are 'trust' and 'respect'.

To really understand we have to stop dominating and start listening. Ellis had to learn the languages of howling and scent and we, who are not intrinsically pack animals, have to learn what makes for effective leadership in the canine world and wolves, closely observed in their natural environment, turn out to be instructive guides. The alpha wolves prove to be, in fact, the decision makers. They are not necessarily the biggest or boldest. It's that "giving the law and making his mates live up to it" quality of Buck's that is really critical. Being 'pack leader' means, above all, that you establish respect. The royal road to that is ensuring that a command is obeyed and it is consistency that matters more than anything else. The key lesson from Shaun Ellis' time living side by side with wolves in the wild is that effective leadership has little to do with domination as such. To be a pack leader you have to lead and lead thoughtfully. Indeed, thinking about the process rather than simply following rules slavishly turns out to be crucial.

From a more academic perspective John Bradshaw is also concerned to question presumptions that achieving pack leader status involves seeking domination, with punishment a necessary accompaniment to the process. The founder and director of the Anthrozoology Institute at the University of Bristol published *In Defence of Dogs* in 2011 and in it he presents an exhaustive account of research on wolves: research which, he suggests, should lead us to think carefully about whether wolves are the key to understanding dogs.

The evidence in relation to wolves is now overwhelming. Until recently wolf packs were mistakenly thought of as competitive organisations. We now know that the majority of wolf packs are simply family groups and, contrary to many notions of wolf behaviour, co-operation rather than dominance seems to be key to understanding their dynamics. This radical change in our conception of pack behaviour has prompted a re-think of the social signals that wolves use. DNA technology, moreover, has within the last decade, forced a reappraisal of the comparison between dogs and wolves because the American timber wolves which have been most extensively studied are only distantly related to the vast majority of domestic dogs.

For Bradshaw it is the process of domestication which is critical and he emphasises that dogs are unique in being the only fully domesticated canid. He convincingly argues that much of what makes them unique was introduced by processes of domestication and that means that wolves should be considered more a closest living relative than a role model. The key difference between a dog and a wolf is not what it looks like, but how it behaves, especially towards people.

Dog pups, in contrast to their wolf counterparts, effortlessly assume a dual identity: part human and only part wolf. That, in turn, means that anyone training and managing dogs with a 'dominance' model is mistaken. Bradshaw looks at the science of dog training, prefacing his chapter title with the question 'sticks or carrots?' It hardly needs saying that he favours an associative, reward based, process of education which aims to show the dog what is required.

Education, which is made possible by dogs' focus on us, is better done if well informed and thoughtful. Better done, it turns out, if informed by the qualities which prove to be essential, rather than incidental, to the processes by which wolves come to assume leadership within the pack. So, the ambition to make ourselves 'pack leader' in relation to the dogs we seek to train is a worthy one provided we do not understand that phrase in the simplistic, and now discredited, way. It's good news, of course, because it holds out the prospect of achieving that precedence in a non-combative way through the consistent affirmation of what we hope for: an agreeable and biddable shooting companion.

THE BARE NECESSITIES

I F YOU'RE FAMILIAR WITH *The Jungle Book* — and who isn't? — you'll know its most celebrated song. Phil Harris and Bruce Reitherman's words, as sung by Baloo Bear and Mowgli, have been indelibly inscribed in our consciousness. Their advice is disarmingly simple. We should "Look for the bare necessities, the simple bare necessities" which turn out to be "Old Mother Nature's recipes".

Could that possibly apply to gundog training? Once the days lengthen and there are more opportunities to do some training with our shooting companions, it's certainly worth thinking about. Is it possible to distil the essence of ideas about gundog training? Is there a 'bottom line' — perhaps a few pithy and time-honoured truths which, if kept constantly in mind, make it easier to get everything else to fall into place? I like to think so.

But before we get onto such truths, pithy or otherwise, it is important to have a clear idea of what we are aiming at. Gamefinding is of the first importance: and that's whether it is producing game for the gun or putting it in the bag after it has been shot. And, of course, the main concern of any shooter or picker-up must be to get wounded game collected and humanely despatched and a competent gundog is essential to that task.

Training a gundog involves a systematic progression through steadily cumulative stages with work on dummies preceding a carefully managed transition to the real thing. Well laid foundations — what the old books called 'yard training' — are absolutely vital. So, whilst we must nurture the hunting instinct, we have also to ensure that basic obedience — sit, stay, heel, the recall and so on — is thoroughly bedded in before more ambitious things are attempted. The whole process has to be one of building mutual respect and experience. The successful training equation — and it's really worth remembering — has to be 'education plus application minus confusion'.

From these general considerations follow two 'rules' of training: and these are the sort of nuggets of truth that we are looking for. They apply to all the elements of the training process, but with particular force to its early stages. They have a 'should be kept in mind at all times' sort of status and they follow naturally from that equation and the all important point about mutual respect.

The first rule is that you must try, as far as is possible, never to issue a command unless you are in a position to make sure it is complied with. It is crucial to developing the sort of responsiveness we are looking for. After all, there's little chance of developing the right expectations in a dog if it is frequently bombarded with a confusing variety that it is able to ignore with impunity. We want the dog's world to be one in which, whatever else is going on, it responds immediately and unequivocally to certain sounds or signals; whatever form the command — and the simpler the better — is taking.

The second rule comes into play as soon as you are starting to make progress with your training. It's all too easy to get fired with enthusiasm and find yourself tempted into trying to see, for instance, how far away — once you have taught your dog to sit to the whistle — you can get it to do it. But obviously, at long distances you are in no position to do anything if the dog doesn't respond promptly. That sort of skill at a distance, important as it is, must be developed gradually.

So the second rule is: never set out to 'test' your dog or over extend it just to 'see' if it will do something. Always be looking to set up training situations that maximise the chance of success whilst also extending your dog's experience. Suppose, for instance, that you are in the early stages of directional training and working particularly on the 'left' and 'right' commands and signals. Sit your dog up with a hedge, wall or some other sort of barrier immediately behind so that the chance of its going back is eliminated. You may only need to do that a few times, because as soon as your pupil has the hang of what is required you can dispense with the prop which has helped ensure that the process of 'getting the hang' of what was required was not associated with any fraughtness. It was consistent, in fact, with another precept which is best kept in mind at all times. Remember KISS: Keep It Simple and Successful.

Nothing succeeds like success and the aim in training, therefore, must always be gradually to extend a dog's experience — education plus application if you like — by steady increments. Confidence feeds on itself and you need to be looking all the time to be ascending in virtuous circles rather than getting swept hither and thither into vicious ones. If something isn't working and you're in a hole, take the standard advice seriously. Stop digging. The response to problems needs always to be: stop and go back to go forward whilst blaming yourself for the need to do so. If your dog seems seriously confused about what you are asking of it then some element of the preparation up to that point hasn't been thorough enough.

Confusion is a word and an experience we want to banish, because if there is no confusion the chance of training being an enjoyable experience for you and your dog is massively increased. And that really matters. Because if you are to enjoy success in your training and build mutual respect between you and your dog it must not only be Firm — that all important first rule — and Fair — proportionate in its approach to correction — it must be Fun as well. Those three F's really matter.

The temptation to rush ahead will always be there. But it must be resisted because, although certain skills are important, temperament and maturity are no less crucial qualities in an agreeable shooting companion and they must be given time to develop. Some dogs, especially well bred ones, may progress precociously in all respects and it is easy to be dragged along at too fast a pace. The safe thing is to assume that developing Responsiveness, encouraging Resourcefulness and, more important than anything else, building mutual trust and Respect (the three R's) between you and your dog is going to demand patience and attention to detail on your part. After all, as someone famously said, 'wealth may enable you to get a very fine dog, but it won't buy the wag of his tail'. Respect, in particular, has to be carefully built from day one: that is to say it has to be earned because dogs are spectacularly indifferent to ascribed status.

As I was keen to point out in my Introduction, nobody has better — or more succinctly — set out what we should be looking for in a shooting companion than Vincent Routledge in his essay *The Ideal Retriever and How to Handle Him* which was written as long ago as 1929. I noted as well that it was in that year that Virginia Woolf wrote in her novel about women and fiction, *A Room of One's Own,* "I should never be able to fulfil what is, I understand, the first duty of a lecturer — to hand you after an hour's discourse some nuggets of pure truth to wrap up between the pages of your notebook and keep on the mantelpiece for ever." Well, so far as training gundogs is concerned, the two 'rules' I have outlined along with the three 'F's and the three 'R's, tick that particular box. They are absolutely fundamental and — forget the mantelpiece — they should be firmly in mind all the time for they truly are 'the bare necessities'.

Make it Firm, Fair and Fun

T HERE'S A NATURAL PROGRESSION from thinking about the bedrock rules that should underpin our efforts to educate a canine shooting companion, because we need to think every bit as carefully about the attitude that we bring to the process. And, when we do, we'll find that there are some beguiling misconceptions out there which we badly need to discount.

We can take a biblical route to the first of them. Corinthians Chapter 13, in the Authorised King James version of 1611, closes with three glorious verses:

11 When I was a child, I spake as a child, I understood as a child, I thought as a child: but when I became a man I put away childish things. 12 For now we see through a glass, darkly; but then face to face: now I know in part; but then shall I know even as also I am known. 13 And now abideth faith, hope, charity, these three; but the greatest of these is charity.

Stirring and oft-quoted: and anyone who has tried to train a dog will know that faith and hope have to be part of the process along, ideally, with the sort of understanding implied by that special use of the word charity.

Indeed, so particular are the implications of that special understanding that it's no surprise that we often translate 'the greatest of these' as love as, indeed, *The New English Bible* of 1961 does. Look up the word 'charity' in the Oxford English Dictionary (OED) and you'll find that it's principally about love of one's fellow-men. Or, more generally, love, kindness and natural affection. That word 'love' is insistent so it's hardly surprising. But I'm going to suggest that if you suppose that love is, indeed, the greatest thing when it comes to dog training you'll be labouring under a misapprehension: big time, as they say.

Trawl through a book of dog quotations and you'll see the misapprehension writ large. Here's Rudyard Kipling, no less, claiming "Buy a pup and your money will buy love unflinching". Helen Exley, meanwhile, expresses the same sort of idea with her observation that "The average dog has one request to all humankind. Love me." You can, for sure, see what they are getting at. But for our purposes that insight of Mark Twain's which I quoted earlier is far more to the point and bears repeating: "Wealth may enable you to get a very fine dog: but it won't buy the wag of his tail."

It's more insightful because it acknowledges that, however much biddability and responsiveness may be there in the genetic inheritance of your dog, the sort of relationship that expresses itself in the wag of your dog's tail has to be worked at. It doesn't just happen; it builds up over time and feeds on all the nuances of your interactions together. That's why questions about the appropriate age to start training are so hard to respond to. It is because key foundations for the training process are laid continuously from day one. How responsive your youngster is to the more formal elements of a training programme will depend crucially on the sort of relationship you have established together.

But is love the most important part of it? Love and affection are all very well. Not least because they are essential preconditions for trust, which matters time and again when dog and gun work together. For that reason I like to think of love and affection as being like credit in the bank. They are something you can draw on when necessary and it's probably true that the greater the depths of your reserves as a partnership the more you have to 'spend'.

There is, however, another key element of trust and its importance is without parallel in dog training so we should never make the mistake of supposing that love is the greatest thing. Like love it has to be worked at. But in line with its significance it is nowhere near so easily achieved. It never results from the one-way showering of affection and indulgence. It has to be mutual or it is nothing. I refer to respect.

Let's return to that book of dog quotations. "A dog", Jane Swan is quoted as saying, "believes you are what you think you are." It would be hard to imagine anything more precisely wide of the mark. Just as money will not buy the wag of your dog's tail your thinking you are the best trainer in Christendom will cut precious little ice if your dog's experiences of your efforts are at odds with your elevated self-perception. Dogs are remarkably adept at that necessary art of bullshit detection. A relationship founded on puffed up self importance is quickly exposed as such.

You might recall that Olympic gold medallist Linford Christie called his company 'Nuff Respect' precisely because he felt he wasn't getting enough of it. Respect is all about mutual recognition: and that's what basics are ultimately about in dog training too. Call it the achievement of pack-leader status if you like: but, as we have seen, we need to be careful about how we understand that as well because the term carries the risk of supposing that it is something that can relatively straightforwardly be imposed.

To see that it can't you only have to witness the difficulties experienced by some who are, or have been, used in their non-dog training and handling lives to issuing 'commands' which subordinates respond to without question. The armed forces are only the most extreme version of this presumption which works well enough in human social settings where rank confers, of itself, a certain sort of status. Note, however, that even in such settings there is something provisional about the status in the sense that someone who persistently subverted the expectations of others would soon find their status compromised. Most positions in society, though, do at least have a honeymoon period during which a new incumbent is given the benefit of the doubt. In gundog training the notion of a honeymoon period is a nonsense.

To win respect in a relationship with your young gundog you need to be aware of its significance from day one. The building of a good general relationship with your pup can at one and the same time be the beginnings of winning the respect that you'll need later on. There is so much in the ancestry that you can build on. Mark Twain, again, in an insight that probably tells us more about ourselves than it does about dogs, said: "If you pick up a starving dog and make him prosperous, he will not bite you. This is the principal difference between a dog and man." Dogs do want to be around humans and working bred dogs are especially keen to please.

We now appreciate that processes of domestication over a 100,000 year span are at least as significant as the fact that dogs are 99.8 per cent genetically identical to wolves. More than that, we also know now that the structure of wolf packs is more complex than simple notions of pack-leader domination allow. Alpha wolves are, in fact, the decision makers. They are not necessarily the biggest or boldest. They, if you like, give 'the law' and ensure that their mates live up to it. Being pack-leader means, above all, establishing respect. And the royal road to that is ensuring that a command issued is promptly obeyed.

So, if we are trying to do the same thing, what sort of precepts should guide us? Interestingly, the OED entry for 'charity' mentions, after its references to love, kindness and natural affection, two other qualities which matter enormously to effective dog training: fairness and equity. They are a pointer to the fact that consistency really matters. Indeed, you can do worse than keep in mind the three F's. The training process must be Firm, Fair and Fun. Firm, first of all, because the dog must appreciate that if a command is issued it must be obeyed. That process is much facilitated if the dog sees the point of the command and the dog is much more likely to see things that way if the whole process is consistent and proportionate: that is to say Fair. The relationship has to be kept in constant repair, of course, and your dog will learn much more readily if the training process is enjoyable. So that's where Fun comes in.

The big message is that the desirable pack-leader status can be achieved and sustained without any recourse to domination. Cesar Milan, in his book *Be The Pack-Leader,* talks of 'calm assertiveness' and that phrase nicely captures the essence of the orientation most likely to succeed.

Section II
Summary

- You may aspire to being your dog's 'pack leader'. But do you understand what that actually entails and what makes for effective leadership in the canine world?

- Have you committed to memory the two fundamental 'rules', 'KISS', the three 'R's and the three 'F's?

- Do you appreciate that in seeking to develop 'calm assertiveness', respect matters more than anything else; and are you clear about how best to achieve it?

Section III

The 'First Course'

Over a hundred years ago H W Carlton emphasised that "the first course is by far the most important." He was right. No time spent on basics like 'sit', 'stay' and the recall is ever wasted. But gamefinding really matters too, so hunting in a controlled manner is vital: and that's a learned skill.

Good heelwork is a 'must have' attribute of an agreeable shooting companion: but it is only the most important of many building blocks which must be well bedded in before ambitious things are attempted.

Steadiness, too, is an absolute must and training a dog which only works when bidden is neither a mysterious nor a difficult process..

Working at what comes Naturally

No matter which breed of dog you shoot with or over, the bottom line is the same. One word characterises the commitment that retrievers, spaniels, the bird dogs and those which hunt point and retrieve, have in common: hunting. Whether it's finding something for you to shoot or bringing what you've shot to hand, our dogs depend on their hunting skills: skills which draw on their deepest instincts.

That word 'instincts' suggests, perhaps, that hunting is something that can just be left to take care of itself. 'Skills', on the other hand, suggests something quite different: something that can be worked on and honed. No prizes for guessing that it's the second interpretation that has more going for it.

It's great to have a dog that is steady and walks quietly at heel; that can be stopped and, when necessary, directed. But if there is one thing that guns who shoot driven game over their dogs will find themselves doing time and again, it's looking behind the line after a drive for a bird that has fallen in cover or tucked up in the ground well forward of the pickers-up — assuming they are well back where they should be. That's perhaps more true of shoots like those in the West Country, but the root fields of the eastern counties have their ditches and dykes. Just hunting our dog quite close to us as we search for something known to be down but not immediately obvious is something we all do all the time. It matters and, like everything in life, it can be more or less well done.

But what does 'more' look like? Well, what's for sure is that anyone who has a dog has a command or signal for it to look, to hunt, to find. Cue 'hi-lost' the most celebrated term in the gundog lexicon, though I've heard others used equally effectively. What matters is what they mean to the dog: whether they mean 'more' or 'less'.

If the answer is 'less' the command will be a cue for the dog to run about, probably covering a fair bit of ground in a haphazard sort of way; avoiding *en route* anything, such as thick cover, which looks demanding; and giving everything it encounters cursory attention. It will be a performance governed by an insistent logic which impels the dog to believe that the more it runs the more likely it is to find something.

The contrast with 'more' couldn't be more marked. We all know it when we see it and we know that dogs with well honed hunting skills put more game in the bag. What we want when we are looking for that elusive bird is a dog with initiative that will stay in the area where we are pretty sure it has fallen and, crucially, 'do' the area thoroughly. That involves being prepared to push into any sort of cover. More than anything else, though, it means being prepared to persist even after a first foray has yielded nothing.

The language of hunting is scent. It's a language we can't hope to learn but, of course, our dogs speak it fluently. And if their brains know how to interpret the messages their noses are conveying they have the capability to learn those fine discriminations which are often the difference between success and failure in gamefinding. Think, for instance, of the bird that is tucked tight in some cover and giving off little or no scent. We know that dogs can be close without finding, but their presence makes the bird move slightly, perhaps, and give off some scent so that, when the dog returns, it finds easily. It has to return though. And that preparedness to work ground more than once, to return to an area which has already been 'done' is what we call 'holding ground' and it's a priceless quality in gamefinding. It speaks of the thoroughness which is often so vital to success.

The regulations for field trials require Judges to take 'natural gamefinding to be of first importance' in their deliberations. The truth is, however, that there's almost nothing 'natural' about it, if by that we mean free of contrivance and just as it comes. Dogs may learn on the job, it's true, but they are more likely to learn to run and run rather than 'hold ground' and hunt in the area we want. When they are getting it right it may look the epitome of doing what comes naturally, but in reality it's the outcome of the care we take early on to introduce and develop the notion of hunting and working a line.

Take any quality which we admire and we'll find, more often than not, it's the result of carefully nurturing, sometimes subverting and invariably re-directing in some way, a dog's natural impulses. What we want is a dog that will hold ground and persist in its work in a controlled way, even though success is not coming its way. So our training needs to include getting the dog used to the idea of hunting ground it thinks it has already covered. A tennis ball or two is all we need. We don't even need to carry a bag: a coat pocket will do.

On walks you can easily periodically hide the ball, call your dog back and hunt it until it finds. Once that is going well you can hunt your dog for nothing. Then when it moves away and begins to take in more ground hide the ball where the dog has previously hunted, pip it back and get it hunting and finding in cover it has already investigated fairly thoroughly. What really matters is that your dog never sees you place the ball. If that does happen it will invariably start turning to anticipate you throwing or placing the ball. Avoid that one false move, though, and you have a fun exercise that is enormously beneficial. Indeed, associate the persistence with a command and you will have something that you can use on retrieves as well, holding your dog in an area at a distance.

Taking 'natural gamefinding to be of first importance' proves to be a vitally important statement of priorities, rather than a literal truth. Natural gamefinding is not something entirely different from training and control. It's part of a package where all the elements are interdependent. As that great hoofer Gene Kelly put it: "if it looks like you're working you ain't working hard enough."

Put some work into hunting and holding ground and you won't have to work so hard on shoot days, forever whistling your dog back to hunt the area you want it to search in. There's real satisfaction in knowing that a piece of ground is 'clean' and you'll certainly put more game in the bag: and there's nothing which is more 'worth it' than that.

Happy to Heel

THERE'S NO SURER INDICATION of a dog likely to be an asset on a shooting day than its being in the right place and at ease, whether on a lead or not, when walking at heel. A dog relaxed at heel proclaims the promise of being responsive in other ways and it's a certain indication that it isn't an incidental accessory to the gun's sporting day. And there's no need for that to be a wildly optimistic dream: so let's begin at the beginning.

First the good news: even if you're not setting out to train a puppy, with the opportunity of getting it right first time; even if your old stager falls far short of what you would wish for in the heeling department, there is hope. Let me explain. We humans think in terms of concepts and so for us 'heel' indicates a state of being close and we use the same word whether the dog is on our left or our right side. Dogs, in contrast, don't generalise. I like to think of what they learn as being 'situationally specific': much more obviously specific to place.

This means that, for a dog, walking on the right side is something different from walking on the left side. So, if you have a dog which walks to heel badly on the left side to the extent, perhaps, that it needs to be on a lead if it is to happen at all, you have a chance to put the matter right. You can, as the Americans say, start over. You have one more chance to get it right. You train the dog to walk to heel properly on the right side using a different command like 'close' and your dog will make no connection between its present exemplary behaviour and its erstwhile unruliness.

The message, therefore, is an encouraging one: it's never too late. What matters, of course, is getting it right and crucial to that is having the attitude of mind that will result in a dog being 'at ease' and even welcoming of the restriction you are imposing. The problem is that the command speaks of control. We speak of 'bringing someone to heel', for instance, and along with that a tone of admonition seems almost obligatory. We want, rather, our dogs to be happy at heel so an appropriately encouraging tone is essential.

Indeed, more than that, we want them to love the lead so that they welcome the chance to switch off and relax. Never be shy of using a lead because it is, if you like, equivalent to slipping a car into neutral. It makes sense from your point of view and also from the dog's, and there is nothing more misguided than the person who boasts that his dog 'never needs to be put on a lead'. Dogs, to their eternal credit, are masters at reminding us of the close connection between pride and a fall. So, using a lead is crucial and having 'good hands' in the use of one is a great help in training a dog, whether young or old, to walk properly to heel.

If it's a young dog that you are training for the first time you will need to accustom it to the lead. Whilst with some dogs that can be easy, with others you get a cross between a rodeo act and a salmon on the line. Patient persistence with the right sort of verbal encouragement has to be the order of the day.

Whether the dog is going to walk on the left or the right the lead must be put on correctly first. You must make sure that the loop is such that when pressure is released the lead slackens and one way to check is to put it around your own wrist and see whether it runs freely in the way required. Once on the dog the lead will be held in the hand opposite the side on which you want the dog to walk, with the other hand acting as a guide for it. The hand holding the lead should be at chest level so that a quick upward jerk is easy. Walk slowly forward encouraging the dog to follow. If it runs forward stop and bring him gently back alongside you before walking again. If it hangs back, or will not move, gradually pull whilst encouraging all the time. After a while the dog will appreciate that being alongside you is the most comfortable position.

Once you have achieved the walk on a lead you can turn your attention to the precise positioning which really matters. Here it can be really useful to walk along a wall or fence so that your concern can be concentrated on pulling and dragging. What you are aiming for is a dog whose shoulder is close to your knee. So, as soon as the dog shows any indication of getting ahead do an about-turn through 180 degrees and accompany it with a slight jerk of the lead and the use of whatever command you have decided on. The key is that a dog that gets ahead should immediately find itself behind again. If its tendency is to lag then you will need to encourage it by tapping your thigh with your guiding hand on the side that the dog is walking. A high head carriage is also desirable and a treat in the guiding hand will invariably achieve that.

After a while, as your dog begins to walk comfortably and consistently alongside you can begin to release the physical contact of the lead. Begin by letting it hang loosely and then, if that works, you can snake it loosely along the dogs back before letting go of it altogether. That way contact is maintained and, although the dog is technically 'off the lead' it will be conscious of control. If, when you remove the lead altogether, you find your dog getting wayward or sloppy then steps will have to be retraced and earlier stages thoroughly bedded in before proceeding to the next.

Once you are confident that your dog will walk reliably to heel in an acceptable way, even if it is still on the lead, be sure to do at least one longish training session — say fifteen minutes or so — which consists solely of the dog walking to heel. This will serve to impress on the dog that walking to heel is not necessarily a prelude to doing something else: a circumstance which the dog might otherwise begin to anticipate. Roaring off, unless commanded, is definitely off-limits once you're serious about heelwork.

Good heelwork has enormous spin-offs in terms of general behaviour and steadiness so it really is worth it. Your dog will, for instance, very quickly come to realise that if you stop it should sit and, if that is being done sloppily or sluggishly, the lead can be used to encourage a more prompt reaction. In short, if 'manners maketh man' then relaxed, happy and reliable heelwork assuredly 'makes' an agreeable shooting companion.

Lining the Brakes

T HINK OF IT AS being like a length of elastic that gets stretched and stretched, often to breaking point, by the excitements of the season. However good the link between dog and handler — and there is no more critical element than steadiness — work in the field puts it under strain. And even the most trustworthy dogs can come to feel that they know best when a bird has been hit: and once they start managing themselves you no longer have an agreeable shooting companion.

To have a dog that does not need to be tethered in any way, and yet does not retrieve or hunt until bidden should be every gun's ambition. And that's because it's not a wild or fanciful one. There is no mystery to steadiness and, whether you are training a young dog or reminding an older one whose standards have slipped, the strategy is broadly similar and a few key principles will see you home and dry.

All dogs, and especially working bred gundogs perhaps, have an instinct to chase something that is moving, capture it if possible and carry it off to some location of their own choosing. Steadiness training is all about substituting for that sequence another which has the dog waiting to be to be told to retrieve before bringing the game tenderly to hand.

Going against the dog's natural inclinations and achieving that virtuous sequence involves breaking it down into its constituent parts and making various triggers like the sound of a shot, or the sight of something flying or moving, a signal to do nothing. Retrievers, in particular, need to appreciate that they are really pleasing you by sitting quietly, taking an interest but not acting on any stimuli.

The first move, then, is to get a dog that will sit promptly on command and not move until permitted. Sit and stay become, as it were, as near equivalent as makes no difference. You will then, as you re-assert the sit command, be able to throw a dummy or tennis ball behind you and, with a raised hand to emphasise the point, keep the dog sitting and congratulate it before collecting what you have thrown yourself. Praise again.

Work on that until you can confidently throw things in front between yourself and the dog and, before long, you will be able to throw dummies around the dog effectively simulating a drive where birds fall around the peg. At this stage a bang or two (and bangs should, of course, have been introduced gradually and very carefully) will add to the realism and emphasise the disassociation we want to achieve between hearing shots and retrieving. Again, collect everything you have thrown yourself and praise the dog: not in a token, but in a fulsome way. It should be in no doubt that it is doing the right thing and pleasing you by doing nothing.

Where does retrieving come in all this you may ask? The best thing by far is if you can just hunt the dog away from the area where you threw things and have it find a ball you have previously hidden upwind, or one you surreptitiously drop whilst the dog is working. Again, praise for success needs to be really positive. All the time you will be emphasising the 'sit' command so that eventually, if the dog is running free and you throw something at the same time as you issue the command it is the latter rather than the instinct to chase which is acted on. You can then move on to calling the dog back to you and throwing something else before sending it for the original retrieve. Everything you do is acting to underline the fact that the dog must follow your instructions rather than its own inclinations: and if it does that praise is assured. Its acting correctly is never taken for granted.

With a little imagination you can vary the elements of the sequence to keep the process interesting and prevent the dog from developing expectations about what is going to happen next. In fact, if there is one principle which is a key to achieving steadiness in any breed of gundog, it is that if you ever get the sense that the dog is anticipating something you must do the opposite. Don't, for instance, get into the habit of giving your dog longer retrieves to collect and shorter ones which you collect yourself to instil steadiness. Because it won't be long before your dog works out that the longer throw is for it and it takes off in anticipation of being sent.

Think about what you are trying to achieve or re-train rather than doing it by automatic pilot and you won't go far wrong. Always stay one step ahead of the dog: accentuate the positive and eliminate the negative and you can have a shooting companion to be proud of. The Holy Grail of steadiness is a process which takes a little while and which involves putting various elements together, but it is achievable.

SECTION III
SUMMARY

- NEVER FORGET THAT 'IF YOU DON'T ACCEPT SECOND BEST YOU'LL GET THE BEST'. SO CAN YOU HONESTLY SAY THAT YOU HAVE LAID SOUND FOUNDATIONS BY THOROUGHLY INSTILLING THE BASICS?

- IS YOUR DOG AT EASE ON THE LEASH AND 'HAPPY TO HEEL'?

- DO YOU APPRECIATE THAT WORK ON STEADINESS NEVER STOPS AND ALMOST ALWAYS INVOLVES SUBVERTING YOUR DOG'S EXPECTATIONS? REMEMBER, YOU ARE RUNNING YOUR DOG: IT'S NOT RUNNING YOU!

Section IV

Building on the Basics: Handling

Marking and memory, which go together, are each a huge asset in any shooting situation. Often neglected, memory is easily developed and the effort is sure to pay handsome dividends time and time again.

The absolute 'corner stone' of any attempt to direct your dog is the ability to stop it and have it look in your direction. Here's how.

A dog that will go out a considerable way on command, which you can then encourage to hunt, is one to be proud of. Not rocket science either!

Thanks for the Memory

I think it's under-rated and under-valued. What am I referring to? Memory: a quality of inestimable value in any breed of gundog, and of particular benefit to any gun who enjoys driven shooting and has a dog at his side whilst at the peg.

There are moral priorities which decree that natural game-finding is of the first importance in a shooting companion, just as it is what Judges should principally be looking for in their assessments of work in field trials and other gundog competitions. If we agree with the late H W Carlton that work in trials is only 'work in the field brought more nearly to a state bordering on perfection,' we'll probably recognise that the ability to handle a dog into a position where it can use its gamefinding skills is a vital accomplishment rather than some fancy adornment which is surplus to core requirements.

Having a steady dog allied to the ability to cast it some distance for game it has not necessarily seen fall, and the ability also to stop and redirect it if necessary, is a great boon when it comes to getting what we have shot into the bag. Those qualities are widely recognised and they are, needless to say, given their due deserts in competitive work in the field.

There's also, however, the question of getting game into the bag with a minimum of fuss: and that's where memory comes in. Why? Well, because it so often makes handling unnecessary. And, for the gun at a driven shoot there's unlikely to be any quality more enthusiastically valued in a dog than the ability to mark and remember the falls of three or more birds, such that when the time comes to send the dog all that's needed is an indication of direction and the rest of the operation takes care of itself.

Because I firmly believe that we must never lose sight of the connection between field trial competition and the priorities of the shooting field it is a skill that I have always taken care to note and value. Indeed, when I look back over the years and recall work that has etched itself into my mind, the collection of runners features strongly of course. But so, too, has work which any gun would relish for its sheer efficiency and absence of any need to intervene in the process. I think back for instance, to a walked-up situation in the 1988 IGL Retriever Championship at Great Livermere. A multiple flush saw two birds and a hare shot in front of the line and another bird behind. The first two dogs took some time, accompanied by much whistling, to find the bird behind and one of those in front. So, when the third dog to be sent went unerringly to the fall of the other bird in front one knew that it was evidence of marking of the highest order, and a sure indication also of an ability to memorise a complex sight picture and know which elements of it had been altered by the work that the dog had patiently watched before being sent. That, in my book, was classic retriever work even though the collection of wounded game was not involved.

It's hard not to mention marking in the same breath as memory for, certainly, the two are inextricably connected. And it is the dog which can hold its mark, or better still, a number of marks despite a delay before being sent to retrieve that looks a class act. Far from being obsessed with the last thing it has seen it calmly adds each new element to its picture of what has happened and waits for instruction as to what to do first.

We could be forgiven for supposing that marking and memory are natural qualities which develop with age and experience. That's true, of course, but it doesn't mean there's nothing we can do to nurture those abilities as the dog is developing. More than that, we can specifically work on such abilities and it is work that pays huge dividends. Memory work involves introducing delays into sequences with which the dog is already familiar. So, once the dog is doing marked retrieves confidently, introduce longer time spans before sending it to retrieve. Then you can throw another ball or dummy behind you and collect it yourself before sending the dog for the first thing thrown or fired. You're making real progress when you can throw two widely spaced retrieves out in front and send another dog — if you're training with a companion — for one before sending your dog for the other; or, if you're alone, collecting one yourself first.

It's excellent steadiness training, needless to say, because your dog will get used to watching you or other dogs 'working' before being sent itself. Remember to vary the pattern. Sometimes send it for the first retrieve thrown rather than the second; or, perhaps, throw two in front and one behind which you collect yourself before sending the dog for the forward marks in sequence. Of course, if you have been 'busting the distance barrier' by working on sending your dog back for a ball or dummy which you have dropped before walking increasing distances further on, you will have been nurturing its memory too because the element of delay is built in; and the longer the distance the greater the delay. You'll be amazed at how adept dogs become at returning to the precise spot where you dropped a retrieve. Again, you can develop skills that will be vital later by throwing the retrieve into some cover and then walking on so that the dog has a more complex memory to hold onto and possibly some hunting to do before finding.

All the time think consciously about how you can build memory elements into the work that you do with your dog. Yes, there will be times when you want to get your dog onto something which has been shot with as much despatch as possible. But, more often, it is the dog that will wait whilst something else happens before going about its work in an organised way that is a huge asset on a shooting day.

There's simply nothing more satisfying than your work coming to fruition after a drive in pouring rain when, with your gun under your arm and water dripping from your hat, you need have no recourse to whistling and arm waving because, with one clear indication from your arm, your dog is on its unerring way to something that was shot earlier in the drive. Other temptations are disregarded: your dog knows what is required and its focus is total. Your painstaking work will have paid dividends and you'll have good reason to sing 'Thanks for the memory' as your dog returns with the bird. It's worth working on: and it's easy to work on.

Stop, Look and Listen

No, we're not talking kerb drill here: it's more a case of the most useful thing you can do with a gundog. And there's a double benefit because nothing will so impress your fellow guns, beaters, passers by in the park or wherever, as your ability not only to stop your dog but also have it look at you attentively and expectantly.

It is with good reason that 'the stop whistle' is considered the corner stone of gundog work, for if working on steadiness is 'lining the brakes' being able to stop your dog opens the door to handling. Never mind that nine times out of ten you will just want to say 'go back' (or whatever command you use for casting your dog out): the point is that other things like steering to the left and to the right become possible and if you get a taste for it who knows where your enthusiasm will take you. But I repeat, and promise, that even if you only get to first base your fellow guns will be slack-jawed in admiration.

Before we get into the 'how' thing, however, a necessary word of warning. To borrow a telling insight from the great racehorse trainer Henry Cecil: "Too much of ought is good for nought." Gamefinding is what matters first and foremost and to do that our dogs must be able to work on their own initiative. There is simply nothing worse than seeing a dog whose handler has got so enthused by their success with the stop whistle that they are forever directing the dog when it should be left to work things out using its own nose.

It is routine to decry trial dogs and handling — until it's needed of course — so it's worth emphasising the Kennel Club's *Field Trial Regulations* are quite specific in condemning any tendency for the handler to find the game rather than the dog. Obviously, we are talking generalities here because there are circumstances — usually when scent is virtually non-existent — where it may be necessary to 'help' the dog a lot.

Anyway, with that vital caveat, it's on to the nitty gritty of how to achieve this miracle of control. And you'll be immediately pleased to hear that it ain't — to resort to one of the more popular clichés of our times — rocket science.

Training your dog to stop to a single blast of your whistle in all circumstances, however diverting, involves making a natural extension of what your dog should already know. Hopefully, you'll already have at your disposal a number of commands which are mutually reinforcing in that 'sit' or 'drop', a raised hand, a shot and a thrown dummy all mean the same thing to your dog.

To add a whistle blast to the stopping repertoire begin with your dog on a slip lead and when it is at heel blow the whistle and ensure that it sits promptly. And bear in mind that you know when you are going to blow the whistle so you can anticipate ever so slightly with the lead and have the dog hitting the deck as if its life depended on it. When you are confident that it has picked up the idea you can try it with the dog close to you but running free. Give the verbal command, raise your hand and throw a dummy into the air directly above you so that it falls at your feet. As you do these things blow the whistle as well. Everything will be pushing the dog in the same direction — into a sitting position. Reward success with praise and concentrate on making sure that the dog not only sits promptly but sits and looks at you.

How to do that? Well, I have already offered a clue. How not to do it was admirably demonstrated some years ago when I judged a working test which was being run by the Italian Retriever Club. One handler had a dog which was by far the best at stopping and sitting in the narrow ride where the exercise took place. But then the dog seemed to be casting its head about and doing anything but look at her. So, naturally, I asked her about it at the conclusion of the day. "Oh," she replied, "when I train I have my husband (a very long suffering Florentine investment banker) in the bushes to the side ready to dart out and give the dog a biscuit when it obeys the stop whistle command. Well there's no need to spell out how misguided that was: it's a sure way to have a dog look anywhere but at you.

We certainly do, however, want our dogs to view the stop whistle in a positive light: that is, as a prelude to being helped rather than in a negative light, as stopping them from doing something they would otherwise be keen on doing. So, certainly in the early days always accompany blowing the stop whistle with making yourself an interesting centre of attention. The best way to do that is to throw something vertically. You can then say, 'gone away' or whatever, followed by 'go back', 'out' or whatever command you have adopted for pushing the dog further out. You have to get it looking positively on the stop whistle.

In time you will want to combine the use of the stop whistle with further commands so the dog must look at you, but don't be tempted to do that until they have been separately learned and are part of the dog's repertoire as well.

This approach to training the stop whistle is almost bound to bring success whereas the alternative strategy of just hoping that the dog will come to see the point of it is a hit and miss affair which will certainly lead to sloppy and unpredictable responses initially, even if it does succeed in the end. Don't, therefore, blow the stop whistle at a dog before it knows what it is in the hope that it will come to see the point of responding. Some dogs are very strong willed and never seem to get the message!

Remember, educating a gundog — and though I have been using the word 'training' it is a process of education we are talking about — is all about making incremental changes which build on what has already been thoroughly embedded so that a sturdy edifice is constructed which can stand all the temptations and rigours of what an earlier generation understandably called 'battle conditions': a shooting day to you and me.

Breaking the Distance Barrier

W<small>E'RE USED TO HEARING</small> about 'the wall' in relation to longer distance athletic events, especially the marathon: it's that invisible barrier, at once both physical and psychological, which seems to make further progress momentarily unthinkable.

And young gundogs, when we're training them, often seem to confront something psychologically similar. But rather than it being a characteristic distance beyond which responsiveness becomes ragged, it tends to be a confidence level relating to distance which is particular to each dog. It will depend on its previous experience and the efforts that have been made to ensure that all basic commands — sit, stay, heel and the stop whistle — are complied with no matter how distracting the circumstances.

That goes without saying. It's no less true, though, that it is a straightforward matter to extend that confidence level: namely, increase the distance at which the dog is comfortable working and responsive to our attempts, when necessary, to direct it. So, if there is no particular yardage that constitutes a barrier, how do we get that responsiveness at greater distances that we are looking for?

What we want, more than anything, is a dog which we can send freely away from us to an area where it will be able to use its own scenting abilities to hunt and find game. And, though it is not essential to teaching it to do that, it does help enormously if the very earliest stages of training included the process of being able to hunt it away from something it has seen to find something hidden in an adjacent area. That becomes the basis of later work with distractions which simulate those situations in the field when we want to collect wounded game before birds which could, in many instances, be picked by hand.

As with all gundog training the process of getting a dog to go back freely involves a number of cumulative stages, each one building on what has gone before in a way that enhances the dog's confidence and trust in the handler. Begin with the simplest element. Drop a ball or dummy that your dog is aware of and walk it away at heel for 30 yards or so before turning and sending it back. Young dogs quickly learn to love this game which can be enhanced by using a hedge or fence line as a guide, in addition to the scent trail which your dog will soon learn to use as well. Try to ensure that everything, including the wind direction, is in its favour and it will start the process of learning that whatever command you use means 'go straight back and expect to find'.

Then it's a case of doing two things: gradually, almost on a daily basis, increasing your dog's memory and the distance it will go back to collect the dummy; and complicating the exercise by building in a distraction element which will have the added benefit of underlining the message you are getting across. Before sending the dog back throw a dummy in the opposite direction and introduce a 'gone away' or 'leave it' command which will be invaluable later. You will almost certainly find that your young dog will become so adept at this game that there will be no need to walk it away at heel and it will nonetheless take a direct line back to the dummy.

And that remarkable ability alerts us both to a danger and

offers an insight which we can use. The danger is a reminder, if one were needed, that we must stay one step ahead and avoid our pupil anticipating our commands. The insight concerns the extent to which dogs seem to rely on pictures and scent memories of the tasks they are given. It's a good idea therefore to get your dog used to seeing you, the handler, as a very diminutive person in the far distance issuing the command which it has learned so well when by your side. That picture is going to be seen frequently and the response must be reliable.

So, sit your dog up and throw a dummy a short way behind it. Then walk a good distance away, blow the stop whistle and use your going back command and hand signal. You may find that, confronted by this new experience, your dog stays rooted to the spot. In which case walk forward and encourage it until the dog realises that the command from a distance is the same as the one it already knows so well. Again, vary things whilst gradually increasing the distances and complexity of the handling pictures you present to your dog. The aim, all the time, is to ensure that the response to the command is the same: to go further away from you.

Since we want eventually to get the same response when there has been nothing memorised to return to we must, again, set things up so that success is likely to be assured and send the dog back for a genuinely unseen retrieve. Indeed, we can expect to go through the same stages relying on the conditioned response which our earlier work has instilled.

All this can be worked on before any attempt is made to engage in more complicated handling at a distance. You can at least have a dog that will go out on command a considerable way and which you can encourage to hunt when appropriate. And that's a dog any gun could be proud of.

SECTION IV
SUMMARY

- HAVE YOU GOT INTO THE HABIT OF BUILDING MEMORY ELEMENTS INTO EVERY TRAINING SESSION? IT SHOULD BECOME SECOND-NATURE FOR YOU.

- WILL YOUR DOG STOP TO A SINGLE BLAST OF THE WHISTLE AND TURN TO LOOK AT YOU? IF YOU HAVE EITHER ONE WITHOUT THE OTHER MORE WORK IS CALLED FOR.

- WILL YOUR DOG GO OUT FREELY — AT LEAST EIGHTY YARDS OR SO — IN THE DIRECTION YOU INDICATE?

SECTION V

FURTHER THOUGHTS

A dog which can't operate equally as well in water as on land is truly only 'half a dog'; and if ever the logic of a situation dictates the approach you should take, work in water is it.

Nothing is more critical or more frequently neglected than the all important 'transition to game'. The 'precautionary principle' applies with real force here: so make haste slowly and the long term benefits will far outweigh any delay in getting to 'the promised land'.

Older dogs have a special place in our affections and, with just a little thought, we can keep them young at heart and responsive.

WATER, WATER EVERYWHERE

SOONER OR LATER — AND, life being what it is, expect it to be sooner — you'll need to recover game from or across water and the competence of your dog will be absolutely vital to the success of your efforts. Indeed, there are good reasons why people say that a gundog that cannot operate equally as well in water as on land is only half a dog. And we all know, because we've seen dogs on shoot days being 'encouraged' across water by having sticks thrown for them, invariably to no avail, that it's not a competence best learned 'on the job'.

A little preparation pays huge dividends so, once the weather is warmer, think about doing some. The question is: how best prepare a dog for effective work, whether it is in flowing rivers, quiet streams, placid lakes or mud bound estuaries with challenging currents? It pays to think it through first. That's because there's an inescapable logic to water work and we have no choice but to submit to its dictates. For whilst much of what we might want to do is really an element in more advanced training that doesn't mean there isn't plenty we can do with a young or inexperienced dog to prepare for those more demanding days.

We want to ensure, as far as possible, that we have a dog that is utterly at ease in an environment which it initially finds strange. Choosing appropriately warm weather and suitably gentle locations take every opportunity to get your dog used to water in a gradual way so that its confidence is enhanced. Think 'nice and easy does it every time'. If possible let it play with a dog that it trusts and which is happy with water.

With luck your young dog will be frolicking and paddling about with characteristic splashy incompetence before it knows what has happened. Generally gundogs take to water quite quickly so a dog at ease in it will be prepared to stretch out for a dummy placed just beyond its reach. And by gradual stages we can encourage it to go a little further and swim a few characteristically head high water churning strokes.

Be prepared for anything though. Some dogs can prove so diffident about actually swimming that they will do anything but take their paws off the bottom. So, be ready to do whatever you can to encourage that first tentative launch: and that may have to include paddling about with your young dog yourself. But, finally, if all else fails you might, as I did once, find yourself having to take your dog to a situation where you can carefully lower it into water which is out of its depth. With my dog it became clear that no amount of coaxing would work, so it was as well that my carefully managed 'learning exercise' was a success.

The dog soon appreciated that the apparent threat posed by the element was illusory and, despite his uncertain start, he went on to win specialist water tests. And that's a lesson that it's always worth keeping in mind. With gundog training early difficulties can so often precede really satisfactory longer term outcomes and slow starters can, with the right encouragement, become beacons of excellence.

The entry a dog makes to water is a matter of the dog's inherent character and boldness. That dog I had to lower into the water to get him started was always careful about how he entered it, for instance. Some people, notably those with breeds which hunt, point and retrieve, are inclined to look on a diving entry as problematic since it is seen as courting danger should there be obstacles hidden beneath the surface. Obviously a careful and steady entry to water can be trained for: but where this is contrary to the dog's natural inclination there is always the danger of creating some inhibition about the element.

For that reason too you have always to be prepared to get wet. We want our trainee to come quickly up to us without even thinking about stopping to shake. Any apprehension will surely communicate itself to the dog and though, at this stage, we are only getting the dog to carry the retrieve a yard or so the seeds of future problems might be unwittingly sown. Why do we want to avoid shaking until after the retrieve has been delivered to hand? Well, shaking is a vigorous affair and dogs often put what they are carrying down so there is the danger of damaging and, perhaps, even losing a bird in the shooting field.

So you have a young dog which is confident entering water and at ease when in it. By introducing a heavier and bulkier dummy to its initial short forays you have helped it discover that by keeping its head down it can avoid all that anxious splashing and make far better progress. That, of course, instils greater confidence. And with that in place you can eagerly anticipate doing more ambitious things when the time comes.

That qualification is a vital one. Resist, at all costs, any temptation to race ahead because your dog seems to be coping effortlessly with the initial familiarisation process. The inescapable logic demands we recognise that with work in water there is precious little we can do if our young dog disregards a command, or perhaps responds in an inappropriate way.

Where water work is concerned, the dog is in the driving seat in the sense that if it chooses to ignore your commands it is simply training itself to be disobedient and that is something you should be aiming to avoid throughout the whole training process. A dog which is frantically hellbent on whatever it has in mind as soon as it gets into the water is of little use to anyone. So the ambition is that any features of handleability that we have on land translate themselves effortlessly to water. Dogs can be stopped, directed and sent for retrieves they have not seen fall and so on. But it is crucial to recognize that there is no point in attempting such things until your dog is doing them reliably on land. In that sense water work provides a testing examination of all your preparatory training.

The recall whistle, in particular, is an important part of ensuring that your dog has no thought other than to get the retrieve to hand. You should watch carefully as your dog is about to leave the water and, if there is the slightest indication that it might be about to stop and shake, be ready with a couple of well timed peeps on the whistle to nip it in the bud.

Otherwise, the principles are those which should underpin all our training efforts. We need to be gradually widening our dog's knowledge so that is equally at home in different water environments. It's fascinating how, over time, varied increments of experience can add up to really significant changes in our dog's capabilities and, as with all training, expectations are hugely important. In fact they are never more so than with water work.

So, from the outset — once the very basic competences have been established — try to engineer it so that all your dog's retrieves involve crossing water and retrieving from a far bank rather than from the surface of the water itself. Why? Well, again, the logic is inescapable. It is simply better to have a dog that expects to have to cross to the other side and sets out with that intention. Because, whereas it can easily be stopped and directed to pick from the water, pushing a dog back which is looking all the time to find on the water is invariably hard work.

Getting the right sort of expectations bedded in before situations arise in the shooting field makes every kind of sense. Water work is a fascinating challenge and dogs which tackle such challenges without fuss always impress — as well as putting game in the bag. Think about what you want to achieve and you'll see the sense of that apparently daft proverb "Don't go near the water until you learn how to swim."

There's Nothing Like the Real Thing

T HERE'S SURELY NO MORE pivotal moment in the career of any young gundog. And yet, for all the preparation we put into basic obedience, hunting and retrieving, we're likely to let the picking of game take its natural course. After all, we reason, if anything should come naturally this should.

And so it can. But often unexpected difficulties arise and that's why we ought — more than ever in relation to this aspect of training — to keep in mind a phrase which we're most likely to associate with environmental politics. 'The precautionary principle' sits perfectly alongside that other phrase which should be uppermost in any trainer's mind: namely, 'eternal vigilance'.

You can expect any gundog to move up a gear or two when they get onto the real thing. The novelty of the occasion is exciting, fascinating and challenging in equal measure; and that's a mix which can easily lead to a dog 'doing its own thing' or, at the very least, something other than what you were fondly hoping for. So it's worth doing everything you can to make this momentous stage in your dog's education as low key and matter of fact as you can. What you'll be aiming for is a seamless transition from a world of retrieving balls, canvas dummies or whatever to one where feather and fur are the focus of attention. A transition where all the things you've been working on — a quick and clean pick up and a speedy return with a nice high delivery — stay resolutely in place as this new and potentially disruptive element is introduced.

Fortunately 'or whatever' adds up to quite a lot: in the sense that, with a little imagination, there's plenty that can be done to ease the transition. And remember, moreover, that moving on to the real thing does not mean abandoning the building blocks that got you to the promised land of work on game. Work on dummies and game can proceed in tandem during the transitional phase: and thereafter for that matter. So what can be done to ensure a 'nothing unusual is happening' reaction to the first encounter with game?

Fundamental, of course, are all the basics: so, with brutal honesty ask yourself the question 'Does my dog pick things cleanly and have only the desire to get them back to me as quickly as possible?' Anything other than a positive response will probably mean that any shortcomings will manifest themselves in an amplified manner when the excitements of game present themselves.

Even if you have answered with a confident 'Yes' bear in mind that dogs can vary enormously in their initial reaction to the novel. Everything from the naturally bold dog which has drive to spare and copes with whatever comes its way, to the diffident one that seems to need reassurance and encouragement before feeling at ease with what is wanted, is possible. Bear in mind as well that such contrasts, marked though they can be, say little or nothing about how effective the dog will be as a working gundog in the long run. But they do mean that assessing carefully where your dog sits on that spectrum of possibility is important, because it will have a bearing on the strategy you need to adopt. And, even if you are confident that you have a dog that will just do it naturally, that 'precautionary principle' suggests that a little preparation makes good sense.

Your dog is much more likely to take picking game in its stride if it has encountered things like it before. You can, for instance, prepare it for carrying something that does not come neatly packaged by putting a dummy in an old shooting sock and having a tennis ball at either end so that it moves about as it's being carried. Other possibilities will suggest themselves. Indeed, if you are so inclined, you can these days buy dead fowl trainers, of American provenance, which have a hard free-swinging head that helps a dog to become accustomed to balancing and carrying an 'untidy' retrieve.

For your dog's first experience of the real thing you will want to minimise anything which might prompt fussiness or apprehension. So, prepare your dog for the experience by adding the element of fur or feather to your training beforehand. This can be done by wrapping a rabbit skin around your dummy or securing pheasant wings to it by means of strong rubber bands. Thus familiarised, you are now ready to progress to the retrieving of cold game. Whilst woodpigeon are likely to be the most readily available a word of caution is needed, because their feathers are very loose and a young dog can easily find itself with a mouthful which will lead it to shake its head and quite forget what it is supposed to be about. So, if you are going to use pigeon take the precaution of binding the wings to the body with a couple of rubber bands and don't be tempted to use the same bird more than two or three times.

Everything we do seeks to build bridges: bridges between what the dog already knows and is confident about and new experiences which, though they will become the world the dog loves the most, initially have the potential to throw it out of kilter unless managed with a degree of care. Wild duck, for instance, are not good things for a young dog to begin on. They seem to be an acquired 'taste' and, though dogs may come to be more keen on them than any other game, few care much for them at first; and the same might be said of woodcock, snipe and corvids such as magpies and jays. So, stick to the tried and tested at the cold game stage and, if that goes well, it should be a short step to carrying warm game effectively.

If you have the sort of dog which is likely to be easily put off, however, you can adopt the same strategy with its first retrieve of a freshly shot bird, whether it's a partridge or a hen pheasant (leave cock birds until hens are being retrieved competently). Making sure there is nothing to distract your dog from its task may mean that you have put your own scent on the bird and this will encourage it to lift it without any delay. All the time we are aiming to maximise the chance that what is effectively a new and incredibly exciting stage in our dog's experience is accomplished with as little fuss as possible: and accomplished in a manner which is consistent with what it was doing when, although its world had game scents in it, the excitements and distractions of the real thing were a promise that it knew nothing of.

When some effort has been put into preparing a dog for work in the field eager anticipation can make it hard to resist getting on to the real thing as quickly as possible. But if ever there was a time for 'making haste slowly' this most important transition in your young dog's education is surely it. After all, think of the time you have already invested. Consider as well the future years you hope to share in the field. A headlong rush seems unthinkable, doesn't it?

KEEPING THEM LISTENING

"Y OU'LL NEVER HAVE A good young'un as long as you have your good old'un" George Meldrum, twice winner of the Retriever Championship and father of Bill who won it in 1963 handling his father's FTCh Glenfarg Skid, used to say. He had a point. After all, we love our older dogs that have grown into our ways and probably developed a fair few more or less endearing ones of their own.

Provided we think of them as 'older' rather than 'old' there's no reason why our relationship shouldn't be attended by elements of mutual indulgence. Pinning the label 'old boy' or 'old girl' on our dogs is, after all, the language of affection and the arrival of a new puppy automatically confers honorary senior citizen status on the well established members of the canine household. But I want to use the term 'older' rather than 'old' because that 'old' label is so often a lazy justification for excusing far too much and, sadly rather too often, for allowing dogs to fit such a description way before their time.

The danger, especially when we have a younger dog coming on, is to give it all the attention and use the 'old stager' in a way that effectively de-skills it: making it a disregarded spectator whilst we work with the young dog and using it to mop up simple retrieves which we have thrown as a diversion for the upcoming star. It is so easily done. We cast the older dog in a secondary supportive role and, in the process, often patronize a perfectly capable companion who will only too readily accommodate to the lowered expectations.

Where gundogs are concerned, though, the advantages associated with getting older are surely so obvious they barely need to be spelled out. Our language is full of expressions which contrast knowledge and that something extra which we recognise as wisdom: and the standard caution about old heads and young shoulders applies just as much to dogs which have to develop keen discriminations in matters of scent and much else besides. As Brigitte Bardot once wistfully mused, "It may be sad to grow old, but it's nice to ripen."

The gundog that has 'ripened' is familiar to us all. With that admirable experience, and the competence that goes with it, is a no less familiar tendency to develop 'a mind of its own'. Extreme versions of this tendency, of course, result in the dog 'which runs itself'. But that's another story. I am concerned for now with the basically steady dog which becomes very confident that it can find things 'on its nose'. The upside of this, of course, and one we rightly applaud, is the ability to demonstrate real gamefinding ability: the downside, if we acquiesce in its happening, is a progressive decline in responsiveness. We are so pleased, if you like, with the 'goods' that we turn a blind eye to the 'bads'.

With gundogs, whether or not physical decline is an aspect of getting older, independence of mind almost invariably is. In many circumstances that is wholly beneficial. We set great store by initiative and persistence: but, as so often, it's a case of 'too much of ought is good for naught' because, if independence of mind translates itself into total self reliance and the disregard of the human part of the partnership that typically goes with it, we are nowhere. For, however much we may admire some of the qualities of such dogs, we certainly do not have an agreeable shooting companion.

Let's try to get to the heart of what I am saying by introducing a word I haven't used until now: secure. It occurs in an interesting observation by a great conductor about his orchestra and what makes it so special. Although Christophe Von Dohnanyi found it difficult to describe the 'Cleveland Sound' he suggested that "It was always very clear, with a tendency to dryness, and perhaps a little too focused on the beat. I have tried to get them to forget about barlines and become more responsive. If musicians are too secure, they stop listening. The great need is to get them to listen to one another."

Substitute the word gundogs for the word 'musicians' in that last sentence but one and you have, I suspect, the nub of the problem with older dogs who have plenty of experience to their credit and are confident that, left alone, they can 'do the business'. They, in short, feel 'secure' and are all too inclined to 'stop listening'. The signs of this are apparent enough, even when training with canvas dummies. Instead of marking the fall of a thrown dummy carefully, for instance, the secure older dog may content itself with getting a general fix on general direction and range, confident that if it hunts the general area for long enough it will succeed. Now that sort of security is often missing in field conditions where birds can plane on considerable distances and complacency is really misplaced. The dog that hunts its way out to a retrieve refusing to pay any heed to help that might be offered wastes time and energy and, if walking up, will probably disturb ground as well.

That is why, with older more experienced dogs especially, periodic refresher 'courses' in basic obedience are a sensible idea. We need, if you like, to listen to each other. The word is in scare quotes, though, because otherwise it would seem too grand and formal. Five or ten minutes a day for a few days can work wonders: the whole point being to put brakes on that process of stopping listening. All dogs, especially older ones, are doing it all the time so never mind if the season is well underway. It's not something that has to be put off until next spring. When it comes to making sure that the dog handler relationship stays worthy of the name there is no time like the present.

The world of field trials has furnished some spectacular examples of the way quality, temperament and, above all, responsiveness can be sustained, and even enhanced, with advancing years. In retrievers one thinks immediately of two dogs: both black labradors. Tony Parnell's FTCh Blackharn Jonty qualified for five successive Championships and was still running in the English team in the CLA Game Fair International at the age of ten. More recently the late Mrs Heywood Lonsdale's FTCh Ulstare Style, campaigned so effectively by John Halsted, qualified for the Championship seven years in a row, twice coming second. And he too was anchoring the English team long after most dogs have developed cloth ears.

Same colour and with quality through and through, but at the other extreme of size, was Robin Laud's cocker FTCh Fenlord Black Beauty, who was working right up to her death on 15 August 2004 at the age of fifteen. A wounded pigeon, shot on the marshes, was brought tenderly to hand with a high delivery: again making the challenging look straightforward, as she had done so often in a career which included six Championship runs: a special life which seemed to have no place for pressure.

Such dogs may be splendid exceptions: but they are, by that very token, a beacon of possibility. By taking eternal vigilance seriously even our older dogs can stay sharp. And they'll thank us for taking the trouble.

SECTION V
SUMMARY

- IS YOUR DOG AT EASE IN WATER ENVIRONMENTS AND EXPECTING TO HAVE TO CROSS ANY STRETCH OF WATER RATHER THAN FOREVER LOOKING TO FIND IN THE WATER ITSELF?

- HAVE YOU THOUGHT CAREFULLY ABOUT THE PROCESS OF INTRODUCING YOUR DOG TO GAME? IF NOT, START NOW.

- HAVE YOU RESOLVED THAT, AS YOUR DOG AGES, YOU WILL KEEP IT IN SHAPE: NOT ONLY PHYSICALLY BUT MENTALLY AS WELL? IT WILL BE SURE TO THANK YOU FOR THE EFFORT.

CONCLUSION

I F, AS I HAVE suggested, it makes good sense to think of the process of educating a young gundog as a journey, it is surely no less critical to appreciate that it is a journey without end. There is always something that can be done. Dogs are not automatons. They are individuals and, like most of us, need to be kept up to the mark.

If you have followed and worked on the suggestions in this book you should be the proud owner of a dog capable of making a constructive contribution to any shooting day. That will enormously enhance your enjoyment of your sport and you will have the added peace of mind that comes from being able to fulfil the ethical imperatives which have always been at the heart of shooting in Britain.

More than that, though, you will have come to realise that you are on a long learning curve: that training any shooting dog involves 'riding a tiger'. After all, anybody can produce a dog which is lacklustre and utterly dependent on its handler: and, equally, it is easy to produce a dog which is wild and which pleases itself the whole time. The challenge, which we all have to take on, is to produce a dog which is disciplined and responsive and yet has the drive and initiative to be the equal of anything we ask of it. The line we tread in seeking to achieve that balance is not a straight one. It has breaks and, at times, it meanders: but as long as we never lose sight of its significance we can hold on to it. So long as you don't expect it to be easy you won't be disappointed.

The balance we seek is going to be a fragile and shifting one. That's just the way it is.

Meeting that challenge can, of course, be fun: as much for you as it hopefully is for your dog. What's for sure is that the learning curve you are on will have taken you into an endlessly fascinating world that, more than anything other, unites the range of fieldsports: the world of scent. That is why this 'conclusion' has to be another introduction, for nothing more fundamentally affects the way a dog works, or can work, than scent. It is the world our dog lives in and for the dog it has a richness that we can barely comprehend, leave alone have any access to. So, if we want to have any sense of what scenting conditions are we have to watch our dogs closely. And that is because, particularly in the case of a stylish dog, it is only their body language, and our ability to 'read' it, that gives us any hope of weighing up the circumstances that we find ourselves in and handling accordingly.

Start to get interested in, and reflect on, such questions and you will find yourself adding 'dog handler' to the description which was previously limited to 'gun'. Your world will have expanded immeasurably, the richness of your sport will have been deepened and the satisfaction that comes your way from taking part will know no bounds. That is a big claim: but experience vindicates it time and again. That is what makes the effort to train a dog worth making. Make no mistake; the prize is, indeed, in both ethical and sporting terms a glittering one.

So, let me conclude this Introduction by returning to Vincent Routledge who set out so clearly the qualities we should look for in an ideal retriever. When it was re-published in 1965 Wilson Stephens added a Postscript in which he underlined the timeless wisdom that Routledge had so eloquently outlined thirty six years before. In writing his book Vincent Routledge had, he said, "wanted to make each shooting day more pleasant for his friends, and their friends, by helping them towards the incomparable companionship of a well-bred, keen and mannerly dog."

That is an admirable aim which I have been proud to share: and if you are now enjoying "the incomparable companionship of a well-bred, keen and mannerly dog" I am delighted and, more than that, I salute you.

LIST OF ILLUSTRATIONS